Remnants

A Collection of Poems by

L. C. Fothe

Second Edition: August 2022

Cover and Interior Design: Creative Publishing Book Design

Table of Contents

Open the Eye of Morning

At morn
Often have I wondered
What is the color
Of morning light
As it rises up the wall –
Brilliance glinting
On gilded frames
Illuminating life
Out of nightly slumber;

Amazement awakens
With contemplation
When time can be taken
In the sweeping of sunlit leaves
From porch and steps
To reveal freshness
In yet another dawn
Presented
For us to feel
Gladness inside happiness
Optimism in promises
A forward sense of

Weddings to be planned,
New sprouts to be planted;

A single shaft
Across the floor
Moves ever so slowly
Creeping in elegance
Reflecting on the varnished oak –
It reminds me
To love
Even that
Which I cannot
Hold
But long
To embrace.

Back to a Beginning

Chairs rock, cradles rock, boats rock, trains rock,
Mothers and fathers rock their children to sleep
A motion repeated so many times cannot be coincidence.

Dive into a swimming pool of refreshing clear water
Relax in the gentle waves of a calm blue sea
Let your mind travel back to the safety of a womb.

Let your ear touch another where the steady heart beats
Feel the arms of safety wrapped around your body
Know the warmth of steady breath as you drift into sleep.

Intrinsic meaning constantly repeating itself
Brings you back again and again to your beginnings
Tethered as we are by our own invisible umbilical cords.

Discovery

It was at a time when I kissed your hand
I knew whatever followed would be amazing
Your stories of life before me enthralled
So unlike my own meager existence
Your desire to listen to my dreams of a future
Wherein we could ride the high waves of life
We could experience foreign places in shared delight
I felt an emotional trust in how we would treat each other
Your spoken thoughts matched so much with my imagination
I felt as if I had reached the first area of true love
As it grew rapidly in my heart as a reality
We took each other to ourselves
We walked beyond fears of past mistakes
A time of inseparable bonding took their place
Sleep came easy on the simpler nights
Knowing we would still be there
With the rising of the sun.

Terrazzo Shapes of Love

Throw a thick rug for our base
Laugh and settle down with grapes
Pour glasses of chilled berry wine
Delicately bite on wedges of cheese
Follow with crispy crackers of wheat
Where will we go?
Where will we take each other's heart?

Terrazzo floors of colorful design
Beckon to our sense of wonder
Showing us the myriad diversities
Found within the grasp of thought
We can find shapes of ourselves
Along with opposites of others
The children of augmenting design
Clinging to the masterful diagonals;

We look to each other for unity
Held together like Terrazzo of desire
Smiles and sparkling eyes
The moments of knowing ourselves
Previews of many years to come

Racing down our private roads
A magnificence of gripping permanence
Like the Terrazzo beneath our lives
We breathe in the sunshine of the day.

The Forming

It feels like slow motion
My touching of her skin
I feel thrilled and afraid
At the same time
Our eyes stare into each other
Travel to intimate places
Her hands pass slowly over me
I hear her breath as our lips touch
We have been patient
We have waited until we knew
Our bodies and hearts could link as one
Words are crude compared to what we feel
Silent connection says it all
We roll into covers as one
Heat rises to crescendo
Beyond simple love is the road we take
A bonding union is formed
Side-by-side we lie together in glistening bliss
No doubt remains as to who we are now.

Love Too

Find a design within a word,
Face to the wind in protective pose,
Power in the knowledge of having,
Remembrances flood every scene;

Tiny hatchlings wait for feeding,
Mothers on wings delicately give,
Rabbit kittens suckle and are kept warm,
In darkness and light is it known,
Human needs arise in identical rows
Cuddling, cooing, crying, craving,
Age being irrelevant – only results of
Love.

Feel it as you will, for passion, for compassion,
For nature, for God –
Entire plethora of life perpetually revolves,
One all-encompassing element persists,
Know it, feel it, revel in it –
The most intangible sought for ingredient
It lives within at every level,
Animates our actions,

Elevates life beyond any limitation,
Wraps us in a full meaning of existence.

Remnants

Scattered were the memories of days gone past
More elements forgotten than remembered
Childhood mistakes, corrections and punishments
Learned sensations of fear and terror from shadows
Being a four-year-old when hardly anything made sense
There were hamsters in a cage on a squeaky exercise wheel
Hearing that female hamsters eat their babies
A new house, new bedroom, Boxer puppies for Christmas

Faces of those around hardly ever stuck for recall
Most of forced schooling stayed in the realm of blur
Pieces of confusion as to who each person was supposed to be
Lack of direction to run when all paths looked the same
Love became the richest goal of meaning
Writing letters of amazing devotion with future plans
Music became its own world of reality escape
Then the full thrust of a work world burst into life
Still remained the sensation of being out of step.

Marriage and beginning a family as an attempt to be grown up
Birth of a tiny human being was the lesson
        of the birth of the self

Memories forged of being clueless while pretending normality
Futility crept in among the mountains of useless training
Reliance on the knowledge of others proved
to be a falsehood cry

The pieces we dragged were the discarded illusions left behind,
A quest for money and material well-being the only goal
Left a trail of questionings pertaining to "why?"
Even the remains of what was said and done became irrelevant
Those who came before should have sent out warning flares –
Should have shared their own disillusionments
In the end the leftover truths of having lived a life
Centered around regrets, mistakes, confusions, bad decisions,
Missed opportunities, fears of success or failure, and loneliness
Perpetuated the myths of what we thought we did not know
Before the setting in of declining into old age oblivion
The remnants can be seen of wasted time and effort
Of a life lived in the all-encompassing shadow of ignorance
Without second chances to come.

Rare Blood Moon

Her eyes flashed the fire of night
Colors of volcanic flow surrounded her frame
Long black hair gave birth to the crows
They flew straight toward the rare blood moon
Quick flying like licorice unleashed
One with sleek blue-black sheen stayed behind
Sat unusual in boldness on a bare broken branch
To watch the unheard of motions below
The rainbow girl gave form to sensual moves
As she danced to a silent parade of sound
The colors flew off her curves in streaks of prowess
Some tried to catch them in baskets of wild mountain rain
She craved a festival in the glade with other warm bodies
Where some said fairy dust could fly in the night
Arms raised above her head in twisted pretzel shape
Her lips parted as she leaned her head fully back
Stars winked and moonlight applauded
Fireflies darted through bushes in frenzies of their own
The night was going to be long but no one was counting
Her presence was not soon to be forgotten

Hard Work Reward

The world seemed to stop as he sipped the cold water
His body's need was the dominating thought of the moment,
Refreshment ran over his parched tongue to an eager throat,
A handkerchief sewn by his wife wiped
across his sweating brow.

Many years spent learning how the ground reacts to care
The plowing, the tilling, the weeding, the planting of seed,
Seeing the mists of water quenching the
catalytic need for release
Watching the tiniest of green sprouts break
forth from the first layer.

Hard work in farming the land was the reward he always sought
Pleasure taken in the nurturing and hoeing
in his time roughened hands
Each day a wonderful surprise of grandiose natural growth
With a counting of weeks until expected
blossoming of vegetables.

Tractors and barns and protective dogs barking is what he grew
up on
Harvesting home-grown produce and gathering
morning eggs his forte

Fresh country air with explosive sunrises for quickest growth
Gentle orange sunsets to signal a day well-spent.

He sipped his cold water reward for labor and toil devotion
On the porch where he could survey the
land yielding its sustenance,
His thankful prayers reached up into the heavenly skies
The handkerchief sewn by his wife wiped across his tired brow.

Fiction is Not Love

How to duck from the spurious words
Aimed at rendering your brain helpless to
Understand the dichotomies between seeing
And hearing is the dilemma of love. Augmented
Descriptions of past accomplishments that none
Present can dispute become the words of insecurity
Concerning lack of perceived victories – victories thought
To lend themselves to the elevating of esteem. It is craving
Deserving of tears for the one resorting to fabrications thrust
Upon those whose only wish is to form bonds of trust and
Belief. This is where the love thrives, not in being convinced
Of events that never happened.

Poet Mine

Indefinite are these words to the unknown poet
You who roamed the streets to capture what you saw

"*Who cares about names*" is what you said
You wanted to be remembered for living not dying

A poet's mind who clung to the sufferings of the lost
Your feet continued their trek to the edge of the sea

Waves rolled their aromas to refresh your nostrils
Memories of baked fish from Uncle Herman's grill popped in

You always wanted to be a poet walking next to a river
Bodies floating by reminded of all things past

When your fingers set words to paper you rejoiced
They let someone else visit your frantic mind

Your need to have others view the world with different eyes
Propelled your mania to broadcast before it became too late

Your journeys to Paris and then on to Rome
Let you drop your words into different rivers of thought

Sense the statues greeting your mind with refreshed words

Send out vibrations in tidy packages of distinct vocabulary

Like sunrises and sunsets, it was truly temporary
What you saw cannot be seen the same again

Oh sweet one, kind one of the the multi-colored thought
Close your eyes and rest awhile in fantasy of oblivion

We will speak again in your poetic language
When you return to the known shores of home.

None Can Know

Under a tree of everlasting shade
Is the stark figure of one
Gazing from a place of solitude
Bemoaning the loss of companionship.

His eyes scour the lives around
Meaning has turned to harsh uncaring
Selfish ruminations want familiarity
The world has been raised askew.

Having been separated out from the herd.
Others seem to not miss his presence
So, how important could it have been
When no longer does he hear
His name being called?

Memories being what they are
To be left where they formed
Attention turns to the bark of the tree
Magnificent armor for what lies within
Not being seen or noticed
Silent vitality is present nonetheless.

Branches, leaves, an open sky,
Fresh air to satisfyingly breathe
Cool grass to be lain upon,
What else should contentment be?

Boomerang

Racing alone
Spinning a flat expanse
Projectile
Looking for a place to return;

Blanket pilgrim
Lies alone
Again
Consciousness unaware;
What he owns
Knowing himself
Keeps him away
From restless walkers
Following
Chasing
Sanity to its brink;

His square root
Holds him erect
Left behind
By those who have
Cruel and undeserved
Inclinations toward pity;

If he drips
He drips on you
Spreading wonder
In consuming feasts
Liquid life
Theorem found true
Another life to come;

Life or religion
Seems to be the choice offered
Steel decisions
Forced into spinning
Good or evil scales weighing;

Again, his sermon calls
Laugh – it's not your face
Cool view through cracked slats
Lettered lines
Sharp pencil glints
Come around again
Seeking their due;

Dead plaything
With doleful eyes
Begs forgiveness
Will you grant

Such request
Or have it spring back
On yourself?

On the Other Side

What is the horizon like
Before it becomes the edge of nothing?

Perhaps it's the ghosts of bears rising up
To fall on their knees in prayer;
Maybe it's where Tolstoy shaves his beard
When *House of Dead* returns

Due to prisoners having moist souls;
It could be where spirit foxes dance
Jumping up out of fog
As they pretend to be hounds;

The clams are safe
Rocking on sand
From tongues linking them clean;

Grasshoppers wish to run
Deep beneath the waves
So their autumn can be dark again;

Something waits at the gate to the sun
Wanting to discover
Does the horizon rise or fall?

Madness resides here
Silently waiting to be understood
Clawing at the other side of the door
Desiring open searching of opposite souls;

Negative energies hold the reverse of living
Yet still alive in a different stage of knowing
Hands reach but fail to touch the horizon.

Transformational Questing

Chanting of a name
Came to my ears
I turned
To find a void
Until floating asterisks
Hovered
Over pink blooming azaleas
Rising from upturned palms;

Spellbound
I felt roots spreading
Rapidly through soft earth
Telling tales
Of truths to be found
Seeking what I know
Knowing what I seek
Description ran through my veins;

I felt a joining occur
Nature wanted me back again
Why should I care
What form I may take?

Completeness is what I sought
Being part of a true whole
Was being freely offered
Silent avenues opened
My name became a sacred bond
I suddenly exhaled oxygen
We were leaves breathing free
I knew the thoughts of many
As i shared mine with them
My new family embraced me
A new existence now bound me to the earth.

Repetitions of War

Fingers fell to languid sadness
Having touched a relic of war
Open fields had repulsively drunk blood
Yet the ground could not name the slain
Away they had flown with cannon balls
Straight and narrow to the ground
Earth rose pink and then again fell
Rust slept within the roots below
Another hour they climbed another hill
Daylight dimmed in their ringing ears
Slowed to dark the horror became
How was it possible to know forward
When present direction was unknown?
Follow the trudge and fear of those ahead
Face in the dirt to hide from screams
Always what is wanted belongs elsewhere
Singing anthems with lopsided tongues
Endings rolled over atrophy
None proved better than the other
We saw photos faded brown with age
Causes that became only words

Lessons had repeated themselves

Again

A learning ran swiftly away unheeded

Until

More wings carried them aloft

In every direction away from Earth

From every period of human cohabitation

With only screams recalled

In repeated histories

Over repetitions of war.

Shattered Illusion

Weariness plows through my skull
    In furrows of disregard
Seeking ways to fill an empty hull.

Diversions steal away time that creeps
    Like tiny thieves hiding bodies
No one ever finds.

Before me appears a figure in brocade robes,
    Three revolving globes in his hand,
Past, Present, and that sought most.

Choose, he says, *the one to break*
    For you wish to believe
There is only one path to follow.

Tempting it can be on sultry nights
    Life being crookedly convoluted
Often wishing to be recreated.

I recognize his face with voice of familiar ring,
    His expression hardens
I cringe as to what is to come.

Fool you are for letting anxiety cover depression

Making you blind and ignorant

Angry over missed love destroying your mind.

Is this really what you want?

The globes spun violently

Until Future smashed to smoke on the floor.

I jump with dismay knowing that was not my desire,

I simply wanted the onslaught to abate –

To allow me not to be afraid.

Are you so ignorant as to not see

I come whenever you call

To demonstrate your need to make yourself bleed.

Blame me not when I appear

I know that you know me;

I am you – and you are me

And together we are fear.

The Caring

He screamed
Someone came
To hold his hand in the night
Thundering turmoil
Disarmed by empathy
Bowed to tender caring
He heard a voice
Advising no thought
Look to silent invisibility instead
Anger slowly gave way
A blank page surfaced
Stillness of breath
Closed a wild eye
Fresh spaces of blankness implored
New chapters be written
In the distance a train whistle sounded
A different kind of scream
Then quiet surrender of forgetfulness descended
The soothing hand of caring
Lifted his heaviness away.

Unbidden

I have heard them in my room
Moving
Walking
Waiting
Featureless faces of white
Expressionless
Somber
Cold
They approach my bed then stop
As if neither of us knows the next step
I close my eyes
It is my refusal
A statement of not being ready
An *RSVP* in the negative
From whence they come
Or where they go
Is the mystery of sighing grass

Visions

In a deep and quiet valley of sleep
Visitors from within the woods came to sit
They spoke in words of a tumbling grace
Visions sprang forth into swift crackling air
Cascading images flowed like sweet cream
Flowers melded into slow warming fires
We saw parades of futures through fine mist
Watched births and deaths of civilizations
They claimed the thrones of builders in time
Showed me flash dances of intrinsic meaning
Swift was the passing of images
Strange people and children jumped in and out of view
Finger snaps of here and then gone,
Temporary existences exposed;
Remember if you will is what they advised:

Hovering above us was a resplendent ark
Vessel of escape from the march of linear time
Asked if I wished to join them in the vanishing
I declined, satisfied to sit at the edge of my dream
Safe in my own deep and quiet valley of sleep.

Renewal

Go to a place sweetly serene
Search within openings of a sponge
Inside the mystery darkness
Awaits my hidden sanctuary
Serenity wraps me in delicate wings
Whispers call forth a warming joy
Sounds of lullabies soothe the world
Calmness spreads across my consciousness
A soft heartbeat serenades my soul
I recall intangible floral aromas
Drifting within a web of smiles
Sunsets cradled in tufts of crimson
Lambs staring with docile beauty
I hug these places to my breast
Unforgettable valleys of quietude
Freedom in a breath of the cosmos
Everything becomes nothing at all
My eyes cruise into smooth slumbers.

Blinding White

Jump and dance to a bright delight
Of having been born as myself,
Seeing in odd ways to match my hearing
I squeeze strange truths into realities.

Sleep calls forth the swift moving dreams
I feel you there by my side again
We hold hands as we race through chilled air
Ice crystals fall from silent eves

A smile and image to a newest memory
Of ethers having sent an angel to me,
Drifting with the voice of concerned timbre
It lifts me up from forlorn to unforgotten.
A cooler white of elegant nothing
Awaits in the distance of noble royalty,
I move forward with discernible motion
Excitement rises within my deepest being

I hear the slow motion of softest wings,
Further into the whiteness we go,
No sight needed to feel the purity
I hug my pillow in joyous exhalation.

In Quietude She Waited

It was in such moment of despair
Her good-byes were weak
Almost voided
Floating in streams of vapid isolation
Not lifting themselves from the turf
Only remaining stagnant in motion;
Her eyes could find no more tears
An emptiness of rooms was palpable
She wanted to do more than stare at her hands
As she sat without inclination to move
The dullness of thickening sludge
Pervaded her mind to a creeping nothingness;
Gone was the comfortable sharing of being,
Lost was reciprocal exchange of living,
Too quiet the stillness of what once was,
Silence being the iron grip of no more;
Bells startled her away from stillness
It was time to follow the polished oblong box
Her feet plodded, her heart wept, the blur began
Words were heard, roses were tossed,
The yawning field of 'where to now?'
Lay before her in its hazy snow-white nakedness.

Finding Forever

A cottage called across an infinite plain
We ran toward a blue essay of mountain heights

The chilling air refreshed our tired lungs
We ran on, hopping over rocks in flowing streams

Clouds formed temporary cities in the firmament
Golden-white rays shot straight to the ground

Birds spoke in their private language of love
We absorbed the meadows in fancy pirouettes

Grasses popped with jumping legs of grasshoppers
A young German Shepherd was heard far away

Purple dandelions lined a path into the forest
We knocked the seedpods into floating umbrellas

Fresh moisture drifted across dappled shade
Cast-off leaves and twigs crunched underfoot

Exuberance filled the open space of our minds
We swam through sweet tastes of the world

A single fabric in a solitary moment of time
The pulse of beauty excited our souls

At last we found the forever moment
At last we knew why we were alive.

Without Words

An amber sky was weeping
Having lost its spinning sun
We stepped slowly into shade
As harbor against the angst –
Together we gathered mushrooms
Beneath black walnut trees
Sassafras grew there as well
Vibrantly alive in its nestled safety:

A whiff of autumn breeze
Passed from fresh mountain greenery
We inhaled deeply and shared a nod
For a cool, dry night of snuggling
Could be felt in our minds;

Our small plaid basket filled with succulents
Necessary accompaniments for a salad to come
Light began to withdraw from the day
We soon headed toward home

A squirrel chittered down its displeasure
Our passing disturbed its nesting security
Warblers' high-pitched calls

For companionship and family to return
Rained from thinning branches –
No matter how many times
We encountered these very familiar sounds
We knew our togetherness was alive
Our living of love was along a singular line,
We smiled our satisfactions to each other
And saw exactly who we were
In each others eyes.

Pristine Clouds

Purple is the field in which we rest
Repose of our loving hearts
Excitation of blossoming scents
Tickles the languid air

Let us rise and run
As the youthful selves we know
Listen to the sounds of our laughter
Toes wiggling in the caressing grass

Drift to the soothing aroma
Rising on smoke of fresh burning leaves
Take my hands to spin around
In freedom's dance of giddiness

Let us sing great harmonies
Each to the other's ears
Close our eyes in contentment
Melodies sustaining who we are

Overhead the skies celebrate
Glorious pristine white clouds glow
Love resides in their billowing shapes
They transfix our imaginations to dream

Let our purple field suffice
Secrets live aloft on those lazy clouds
Hearths and fresh-brewed coffee
Await in the next blinking of our eyes.

Pointless

Bereavement is the bloodstain
that never washes out. Grief follows
a path of trance into deep crevices
clinging to walls of desperation
to comprehend the will of God.
Where has gone the one who left?
We hope to know such prayers are truth
Dry tears remain a staple of the living;
Prayer on knees offered for solace;
A candle is to be lit in a small red jar
for the memory to remain blessed
but there are no more real candles
only flickering electric bulbs of falsehood,
Giving off a light of emptiness,
They have not the power of comfort.

Where Are We Now?

It was at the cusp of oblivion
They huddled like kittens in the dark
Waiting for an unknown shuttle
To ferry them into vast bleakness

Disassembled to filtered purification
Drained of active impurities
A future warned and foretold
Ignored when opportunities thrived

Abrupt endings came to pass
Unexpected finalization threw down –
The dance ended on slack marionette strings
The stage of forgiveness passed on the map

Their eyes stared into nothingness
A platform began to move beneath their feet
One by one they felt each other leave
Tumbling in acrobatic flail
The voracious appetite of elsewhere
Satisfied itself once more

Passing the Inevitable

We rode on past the cemetery gate
Blindered horses kept us straight
Brisk our passing
Rustled silvering leaves

If waited long enough for passing by
Difficult discernment
Where lies such granite and marble
Holding the helpless down

Once was heard the voice of death
It beckoned from the void
Shutters slammed themselves shut
Darkness awaited the light

Listening never shuts itself down
The bells are being heard
Perhaps we should wish to watch
Monogrammed shovels in the night

A Lone Feather

Feather fallen to the ground
How came it to be here?
Aloft! Aloft! Should softness be
A gift for my mind –
A soothing touch for my brain –
I pick it up and spin it
Fascination in full gear
Sheen and smoothness
Captivate my mind
Transporting me to another place
Of solid perfection –
I feel love
Subtle grace
In gray and white
Inviting me to know
The secret of belonging
As one of many
Yet intimately independent
Knowing it is I who could fly
By the gentle feather in my hand
Giving me a lightness

I could find in no other way
It is a dissolving moment –
It is
My private moment of illicit flight

When No One Answers

It was once there an old man lived
Elongated shack from obtuse angles
Picture perfect not the scene
Doves pecked seed on the ground

Other worlds turned remembered
Notated in printed form
The air had changed to chill
Closed curtains hid the truth

Sometimes out the door he cried
Begging someone to answer his fears
Being all alone held the worst terrors
Soon he would forget and head back in

Other calls came from deep inside
Quiet summonings of loneliness
Finally tired from lack of response
The voice unwavering faded away

Let Nothing Disturb You

In the midst of stoic tragedy
Comes creeping tall doubts,
Eyes closed with blank screens ahead,
Every fear of the dark awakens;
Where now do the swans wait,
Swimming in majestic pride,
Listening to the turning of the wheel
To bring their charge for escort?

Spinning wildly in the centrifugal well,
Against the wall in helpless sprawl,
No strength to reach the hanging rope,
No one else to pull the lost up and away;
Murky water below smirks at desperation,
Despair being its moist tasty delight,
Waiting for the centrifuge to falter,
Just enough for glorious *slip-slide-fall:*
Yet the patience bell continues chiming
Ears can hear the corrective tones
Waiting exerts its claws of difficult demand
The light without shadows will come

Inadequate

In her days of death, it seemed quite clear
    The ways and means of life around
Her bed in wisps of passing gear,
    Those to be gauged by weight and pound
And their rate of buzzard's descent
    So like winter hung dead on a tree.

In smiles they whispered of decent
    Deeds she did for them selflessly,
Then saddened their eyes, sagged their stance,
    And stayed a good three feet away;
(She'll steal your life given the chance)
    But *'We love you,'* is what they said.

She knows the thoughts well, for her own
    Were theirs when listed as 'living.'
Now sadness dictates from the bone
    That she must do the forgiving,
With all the flowers, cards and lies,
    The one thing she needs, they can't give
A warm hand to help break the ties
    So she can leave
        And they can live.

Betrayal

Manacles of dread and despair shackle my wrists
To bind me to my inescapable self
Knowing death is salivating deep within.

Never did I wish to anticipate the arrival
Of inevitable endings creeping through me –
To say I am afraid is woefully inadequate.

Pain is the torture that allows me to torture myself
I scream in my mind where no one hears
Ordering and begging for it to stop
Like screaming into a vacuum where there is no sound.

It's my body betraying itself by its own design.

Where I Am

I became lost
My mind sucked in dry air
Running feet slammed into triggers
For why I ran in the first place.
Sleep as a hiding place stayed at bay
Tortured me to roll and turn
Over and over again in frustration
My body felt so different
Not at all the body I knew
A home where the lights
Wouldn't turn off
A continual wakefulness
Prayer turned begging
Into selfish pleas
Like slicing open skin
Trying to pretend
Nothing happened
Where and when
Will oblivion bring solace?
I wished to hide from myself –
Every corner too well-lit

I was without escape

Now I am where I am

Helplessly

Watching the hours tick away.

Lost and Found

There's certainly something to be said
About who you used to be
When that is not who you are
Anymore
Thought changes its own texture
Struggling toward recognition of pattern
Groping in a mire of confusion instead
Concentration
Somehow saving what's left
Urgency
Swinging on the vine of fading intelligence
Wrestle to sing songs of triumph
Wave flags to find where you've gone
Lonely places hidden from your own view
Pop in and out like fun house mirrors
Warping knowledge into befuddled amazement
Recognition
Disappearing in cataract haze
Dreams
Hoping for less disaster
Knowing you have found the corpse
Of who you once were.

Who Can Know the Belief

The cathedral sagged from side to side
No more bribes to be had
The doors are massive and dark
Smallest of the meek struggle to get inside

Many ascend the long narrow stairs
Searching for what hides from sight
A loft – choirs singing formulated verse –
Smooth wooden pews beg a warm presence

Mixed eccentricities sit side-by-side
None know what the other thinks
Echoing sounds concerned with souls
Searching for any who may actually hear

Appetites

In school I studied
Female anatomy
    Other guys took shop

She turned in place
Smoothly backed
    I tied the apron string

The treats enthralled
Cupcakes and cinnamon buns
    Pastries filled with delight

To choose, to choose
What to eat first
    I greedily bought it all

At Peace

The wine glass and I stare at each other
    Chardonnay and color of my thoughts match
Hummingbirds with yellow butterflies
    Glide and flit through the convex curves
Tiny to large to small again in a flash of dance
    Disappearing into their instant of being
The porch is cool, the breeze is slight
    Wind chimes tinkle in graceful chorus
Rabbits dart under the old wooden fence –
    A red-tailed fox must be roaming about
Wisteria vine climbs the posts like aged fingers
    Rich purple and white flowers carry lizards aloft
Blackbirds pass in thick flock overhead
    I sip my wine to the comforting peace of it all

Grasshoppers, Crickets & the Way Home

Silhouette against the horizon wall
Day and night careening into each other
Bare feet over dirt paths passing
Vineyards of *sauvignon blanc* on either side
Slow walking away from a day in the fields
On a *quadrille* of workers harvesting grapes
Bending, snipping, carrying, basketing
Ripened clusters of delicate hue
Three miles gone with two to go
Cricket and grasshopper chirps of song
Large orange-pocked moon lights the way
Smiles and dances cavort in the mind
A tiny baby hand wrapping around a pinkie
Veal stew at home calling strong ahead.

Here I Am

It's a playpen in the mind
A square of barred containment
Wherein carries great solitude
No one else knows the games invented
In that small world of no escape

Sometimes helplessness prevails
Events spin wildly out of control
Voices raise in frustrated frenzy
A storm carries away the weak and the slow
All sense of direction is lost

The airport roads are closed
Runway lights are turned out
I wave my arms in desperation
But to no avail
No one is coming to my rescue

I wish to be saved from inconsistency
My mind plays sadistic tricks against me
Anger clouds any semblance of intelligence
The lips form sounds uncomfortable to ears
I no longer want to say things I will later regret

They seem like lies invented to hurt someone else
When all I did was hurt myself instead.

Steps to Redemption

Pictures in her mind carried sounds
Voices were unforgettable
Words still stung long after their departure
Regret canceled innumerable good deeds;

She retraced steps in concentration
Wrote tiny notes of apology
Stating what should have been done instead
Hoping for forgiveness of her ignorance.

She wanted her mind of regret to dissipate
A redemption was her only goal
To unburden others from distasteful memories
To clean that which she had soiled.

She knew a hand, a touch, a kindness
Could have served up slices of sanity
To forgive a memory
That never should have formed.

How it Goes

A new breed came to be
Launched from a sad man's eyes
Tight was the focus
Soft the expression
Beseeching the brow
Knowledge locked inside
Books abandoned
Tears of possession left behind
Meanings crumbled
Loves crushed and lost
Plans dropped into emptiness
Life lived out
Future became the past
No one came around anymore

A lighter flares
The cigarette sizzles
The one who puffs
Does so for memory's sake
Evening clouds move away slowly
Orange sun turns to gray reflections
They remind him of his own fading light

Not long will his presence felt
He feels like the singular frog
Jumping to the curiosity of a window pane.

Imitation is Not Flattery

How true the words of change –
Who were you before you awoke?
A stream of teaching taught who to be
Where did the original version go?

The world has come unhinged, they said
Never was it hinged in the first place
You watched in bleary-eyed stare
Waiting for alignments that never came

Trust fell away like hair from the scalp
Certainty was a just a library book
Instead of being filled you became empty
Imitation – the hideously lame horse

Now you have become an amalgamation
Mixed and stirred to gross imperfection
From mating extreme opposites of inconsistency
Another generation brought you exactly nowhere at all

Age insists something was dangerously absent
Confusions grumble in the leftover mist
Paths followed led to desolation of falsehoods
Old instructors now hide in silent graves.

Rejoice when the emergence comes
Run to embrace the hidden talents within
Marvel at your escape from past indoctrination
Don't be afraid of the mirror anymore.

Somewhere Better Instead

I felt the world reach into my soul
Searching for a truth – *the* truth
That could pluck me away –
The solo actor in the play –
Was it jealousy or fascination
Causing the search over miles
Always seeking an answer as to *why?*

Stating I could stay
If only I would stop the vigil,
Walk further on with my heart
Love is the sharing I wish to give
A touch serves the energy craved
A look possesses the magic soughtk
I carry all that I thought I knew
The burden is growing heavy –

One hand reaches up
The other reaches down
I have no wish to dangle
Let my wings make the choice
Carry me to the stage of desire

Rally around a joyous Maypole
Dance to the rhythms of another

Forget the terms of temporary existence
Dance to the rhythm of being whole
Sing to heights of having met someone I know.

The Nightly Out

In the needled darkly dead
Carousing tigers pad instead
Your lions bow their lonely heads
Out from bridled sickly beds

In the ordered spryly shy
Imbuing creature' cries imply
Feeding dishes turn their eyes
Out to spiraled thickly whys

Down a bottled badly dread
Arousing panthers strip a thread
And many slippers buy the breads
Up from sparkled crispy spreads

Over hobbled manly fly
Inviting sewers signal buy
All the wallets beg replies
Under startled limply lies

In the condos hotly still
Distracting stardust hits the sill
While all the promised yank their thrills
Out to harbored vaguely chills

In the humbled lonely cage
Surrounding players peel no page
Cublings know the secret stages
Out from spindled nightly wages

Empty Houses on a Hill

Exposed and naked for all to see
Abandoned to silence of irrelevance
Yet screams resound unbidden
Wallowing in a pit called alone
Empty shells devoid of purpose
Houses no longer home to the viable
Deterioration lets slow cracks widen
Windows display sad countenance
Occupants of each long gone
Embedded memories fossilized;

Where once laughter and singing
Sounded in normal life's cadence,
Each domicile a stage of acting out
A rhythm of years' repetition,
Once peopled in love, affection, learning,
Remain fallow like uncleaned planters
Holding stale dirt discarded;

Only one watches the disappearing,
Fading sun darkens this forgotten display,
Empty houses begin releasing their dreams

Into a stilled air of nowhere,
Fulfillment and implementations left behind
On frozen wheels of former youth
Fading, fading, fading,
In dulling curtains of grey,
None any longer climb the hill,
No one remembers why that is,
No one will be returning tonight;
Quiet. Quiet. Do not disturb.

Who's There?

PHASE ONE

**In a solitary hall of mirrors
I stumble into reflections
Unrecognizable
Disjointed and fragmented
Glamorous lights extinguished;
Too many glinting images
Begging to be reassembled;
I turn frantic
Vacant eyes staring
Thin shadows
Slip between whispers
Jagged edges
Of sharpened glory
Tease my furtive vision;
Fingers to lips
Silence forgotten stories;
Lost within reflected breath
I search elongated elements
Images I should know
Somewhere deep**

In many replications
Lies a beginning
And an end
If only I could remember

PHASE TWO

Lost again in campfire glare
Owls watch and munch white moths
The whining high whir of katydids
Defines a tightening grip of darkness

Transfixed by the smell of earth
The smoldering popping of flame
I hear life rummaging in undergrowth
Slow snapping twigs of the curious

I wish to know what lies in darkness
Watching me though I cannot watch them
There is only my flickering circle
My dome of physical consciousness

Together yet separate we are nature
The fire flares at my floating thought
I am only an outside visitor
Waiting for a new morning dawn

PHASE THREE

No matter where the finding occurs
There is forever a craving to be known
As a discovery of the complete inner depths
Racing through the forged raceways of the brain
Where the mind projects itself on screens
We view with straining eyes.
Not always can we ascertain who it is
Inside and outside get confused
As to where we wish to go
It would greatly clarify the need to proceed
If we knew who is really there.

Maybe Tomorrow

In the long before
(Following after awhile)
Crispy George scurried across hot dry sand
To reach the weaving edge and ease into coldness
Snapping Sally had not yet caught on,
Still lifting claws skyward to attack the boulder's
Crawling shadow.
The overturned hull of a rotting forgotten boat –
Any name disappeared with most vestiges of paint
Scrubbed clean from the sand encrusted winds of night.
No one seemed to ever know how these beach relics arrived
Or even when – just things that are not until they are.
Blue, blue, blue of a completely cloudless sky perfectly outlines
Seagulls scanning the matching water while crying their hungers
As if the fish would jump out of the water to
make their presence known
The sleek white wings of the gulls force our
eyes to follow their grace
In our amazement over such ability to stay
aloft on simple air currents
We often wish we could experience the feeling of such freedom. –
To know the magic of learning how to accurately see sideways

Far out on the horizon, a sailboat in full colorful sail moves slowly

Looking like a simple toy on the edge of the world so far away

And when it turns it actually does disappear as it falls off that edge

Vividness keeps its finger on my heart so I never need be alone

Maybe tomorrow I can climb a tree to see
another part of the world

I may have missed

Knowing the Glory

Many are they who come to see the faces
Golden arms raised in supplication
Paintings blasting their color across the sky
Azure squeezing tight to billowing orange fire
Divine intensity being showcased
Rays of precision spiking through jubilant clouds

Power behind the display presumed
Fertile provider of living existence
Known through its implied meaning
Insurmountable our tainted comprehension
As we watch the creeping fall of descending
The waning ebb of a brilliant day being wrapped
In ebullient salutation to the coddling pall of night

Second by second a dimming seeps across time
Fading – Fading – Fading
Our longing triggers us to know
Deep desire calls forth
Wishing to follow the secret down
Eyes fixate on that life behind a life
The loss feels as palpable

As it is inevitable

Then in a wink

The world has been anesthetized once again.

Forgotten Castle

I

The empty steps of Castle Yore
Are yearning for the feel of feet
Upon their grass covered eaves
From which the men did retreat.

Once these steps were walked upon
By the most gallant of knights
But now only the wind shall pass
Affecting not a thing in sight.

Still in the dank darkness of night
Do live these great men
Whose swords and brilliant armor
Are raised to fight once again.

'Forever onward!' is their cry,
As they march across the land
To regain their long-lost Valor
By lending a helping hand.

II

A sentry is at the gate
Of the victors' entrance

For the valiant warriors
Who return proudly with their lance.

To us the air is musty and damp
To the courageous it's as fresh as Spring
Finally, they can return home
To hear the chapel bells ring.

They march through in sagging lines
Exhausted and in need of rest
But no one dare deny
That they are among the best.

Before the battered armor is removed
Summoned are they by the king
To join the festivities for them
Where half-clad women are to dance and sing.

III

Enter all of the glorious knights
Where the dark, bare chamber walls
To them, look as home,
Are damp, crumbling, and ready to fall.

'Let the festivities begin!' cries the king,
And all do rightly obey
As the flailing silks and jewelry
Fuse into one vivid and colorful array.

The weariness begins to wear away
To make room for well-deserved reward
Of enjoyment and mind fluttering music
Only for which they can thank the Lord.

Hours and hours pass swiftly by,
Leaving everyone asleep or drunk,
The view is now fading,
Back into loneliness the castle has sunk.

IV

There's a short moment of echoing whispers
As the sun rises up the tower
Then again all becomes still as death
In this, the pitiful closing hour.

The walls have stood and will forever
To house the great warriors of our past
From the cruelty of our modern world
In which they were forgotten so fast.

Into the sky rises this castle
To stay in heaven forever more
As an unseen beauty and wonder
Of which there is only one
    Forgotten Castle Yore.

Ride the Thunder of Bliss

In the night long thunders can roll
Blindness has a sight of its own
Feel the growl and tremoring ground
Hear dark sorrows on the prowl

Rains fall slow to quench a thirst
Mackerel gills anticipate clean air
Deeper seeping draws a trickle down
Sightless worms wallow in refreshment

Splash through cups of hollowed impression
Laugh for a cool reminder of birth
Ambling thoughts focus in the moment
Fascination fixates on miracles from the sky

Fears wash themselves away with sound
Thrumming safely against resistant roofs
Outside aromas waft drifting sweetness
This night harbors no ill-intentions

Stars beyond clouds watch their creations
A twist to a turn peeks through soft gaps
The moon winks its magic soon to come –
That which passes is irreplaceable

What to Seek at a Waterfall

Feel the chill of refreshment
Splash in the mists of nature
Search smooth stones of time
Find the love
Waiting in the waves
Dive together in the depths
Of discovery
And satiation
In the ballet
Of cold water falling

Ride the myths of youth
Imagination the rider
Down a grand waterfall
Roaring in power
Raw in its appeal
Crashing
Into foam
Dissipating
In the exciting
Glory of endless flow

Thrilling and soothing
Hypnotized by sight and sound
Amazed by every aspect
Strong wishes to participate
To feel the rush of speed
Weightlessness of the fall
The spreading of self on waves
The calming into a pool
A knowing of exactly
Where you have been
Adventures lived
Travels to define
Who and what you are.

Glory of the Muse

Cold is clear sparkling water
Leaving smiles in its wake
A fountain's flow bringing pleasure
To the brow of a questioning one

Pages flap and flutter openly
Telling of glory and slaughter
A book borrowed to fill in time
A bench for sitting to watch the passings

Shadows of the birch cool the air,
Bumblebees stop, look, and fly on,
Happiness seems tumultuous
A place of contemplation is a rarity

A journal calls for words to be inserted
Tiny thoughts of grasping time of living
Poetic in their finding of the Muse,
Weavings of the soul revealed.

Short glimpses perhaps will live on
A reason left behind to be found
The air is fresh, the words are clean,
A folded life is neatly placed.

The Silence of Waiting

Behind a drapery she pulled aside
Hidden life was revealed
Down sidewalks of utilitarian value
Disappearing around corners like shoulders
Rounded to the left and right
People going about wasted time
In unrealized frivolities;

A reflection in the glass
Resembled someone she once knew
Before the clamp of abandonment closed
Now an imitation of former existence
Almost unrecognizable,
Recalled;,

She will venture out
Follow familiar streets
No one will acknowledge her presence
As she will ignore theirs
Consciousness lives alone
In a vat of vast avenues
Branching beyond elastic realities

Stretching itself
For a definition
Comprehensible
Purposeful;
Once again she will purchase satisfaction
For what she craves
Return home with crispy packages
Place items in predetermined order
Close cabinets like secrets
Sit alone
In wooden spindled chairs
Study roses in a cool green vase
Waning petals of meaning
Reflect more than is seen
Daylight pulls down its drapes
In silence she still waits.

Small Opinions of Doubt

**Where are we to go for adventure?
In which section resides solace?
If my next breath is silent
Will I feel the fall?**

**Strictly a force of looking inside
Jubilant voices find myself
I see I try for closely monitored patterns
To plan next steps to be taken.**

**Speak they do in coded whispers
Knowingly smart
A map gets laid out of destinations
Too many voices vote on what is real.**

**Who ever knows who is speaking
Conscious deduction
Outside scoffers deliver disbelief
Concerning the more-than-one inside.**

**How can I hope to choose what is right?
No exact guideposts bring clarity,
I move forward in blindness
Wishing choices could be so much clearer.**

A Hole Too Deep

Men drilled for years
further down
and further still
to see what they could find,
cutting their way through pretense
like slicing into soft flesh
scraping true bedrock
where purpose
wanted to be found.
Silver knives darted across
in waves of a raucous river,
molten water
where it should never be
raced to a hidden shore;

Voices from the deep earth
worked their way up
through cuts and fissures,
openings never meant to be
revealed –
Faint yet distinct
Moaning

Wailing
Screaming
Calls of anguish
and despair
begging for relief
escaped
from the imprisoned heat –
night upon night
day after day
imploring
human voices
rose from the tiny abyss
Even skeptics
non-believers
scurried away
from the impossibilities
coming from deep
inside
the lower
unknown
forbidden
earth

Drills broke,
heat too strong,

workers refused to return,
governments gave up funding –
fear or economics?
No one knew.
The hole that never should have been
Was capped.
Some claim
hoax
recordings faked –
Facts or battles
against religion?

Work sheds
and expensive equipment
rust in desolation –
Abandoned.
But
memories
of those hideous voices
in great misery and pain
could never
be erased.

Answers Awaited

Seeking directions through tears
Where dissolved my paths away from here?
Rabbit holes embrace darkness
Foxes in dens await the hunt
Is faith true belief or simple desperation?
The next step black or white?
Changes bring irascible tendencies
Roadblocks with nothing on the other side
I search to find future knowledge
In acknowledgment of past currents
Perhaps someone knows answers eluding me
Maybe someone else knows the secret
What I discover disappoints
All the paths already repose before me
Thought warps wisdom into foolishness
My tears continue to fall

Toys & Games & Fantasies

Times of playing have meanings of their own:

Adventure

Glee

Undeniable satisfaction in the actions;

Moving little pieces on a game board,

Battling with cards for highest pips,

Bouncing a ball to pick up star-shaped jacks;

Swings and slides and carousels,

Running fast and jumping ropes –

Laughter, joy, or exultation,

Carried us away into hidden realms

Where make-believe was as real as breathing

Imagination was the true meaning of life.

Smile, remember and dream,

Touch the vibrant friendship of youth,

Feel the toys defining who you are,

Lounge in the embrace of the

Indelible

Forever

You

Be the Freedom

Listen to footsteps in heavy march
Others follow where you have no wish to go
Creativity calls you with irresistible charm
Imaginative blossoming fills a romantic mind.

Constant badgering wants to be avoided
Those close to you rant over ways to succeed
Exhaustion creeps its way over tension
Find a hidden escape through which to flee.

Your art is the place in which to live
Only you can have the visions you do
Capture as many as you can to bring to life
Let go of need for approval or encouragement.

To taste a freedom from what is known
To bring reality to gripping imagination
You are the gift to the gift of creation
Display the meaning residing beyond the clouds.

Where is the Sound?

The morning broke over the earth crisp and clear
For my exhilaration
After coffee, I slipped into my jacket and
Headed out to the barn.
Although the morning air was refreshingly brisk
There was something that struck me
As being strangely awry
A weird realm of uncustomary silence
Enveloped the area
As if the world simultaneously stopped moving
Quiet rode across the air with an eerie stillness
Where was the sound?
The mind cried out.
After a few long moments, the usual noises returned
But my mind pondered how the silence came to be.
The mystery stuck with me the rest of the day.

Appetite for a Future

In a long ago state of prevailing thought
Mountains were the personification of permanence
Statements of grandeur that held open the gateway to patience
To be looked upon with amazement and distant respect;

Up against their stiff-sided granular height
A person comes to know their own insignificance
Yet still the driving desire to climb calls urgently
To rise above that which is desired to be left behind;

Erroneous assumption of needing to conquer
When no such preposterous event is present
Up close brings awareness of skin-shredding roughness
Curiously oblivious to the blind beggar at its root;

Still a peak awaits if only in a remembered photo
Cloud rings and snowcapped infinite glory shines
Dreaming continues of rising anxiously aloft
Many feel compelled to lift themselves higher
Belief fills the air of wanting to be more than they are,
Climb on toward what could have been,
Climb on.

Unity

He stared up at the exquisite night sky,
Onyx with imperial specks of brightest white,
Alive in mystery of viewing –
Alive in pools of secret revelation.
Always did the view touch his soul,
The vastness defying full comprehension,
To be a part of such magnificence,
He was a child on a sea of understanding.

It was the fabric of dreams wrapped in eternity
Into which he sojourned,
Neither feeling fear nor loneliness,
Experiencing the thrill of ultimate birth
Within an almighty power of creation,
Not needing to be tactile,
A direct connection to his willing mind,
Instinctually knowing he was staring into the core
Of that which defined us as part of a single entity.

Imagination drifted between the stars,
He sought a meaning to his wonderment,
Scientific explanations failed to satisfy cravings,

He wanted a way to get closer,

To feel the true immensity of powers,

He wanted to know for sure who else was there.

No Label Suffices

In a singular gleaming drop
All things called colors swirl,
Counting my altruistic meanings,
Then fall to unrelenting gravity.

Creation rests lively before me,
Changeless in calm evolution,
Speaking in tongues of antiquity,
I listen in awe of silence.

Can my existence be felt?
Can I feel other existences?
Separate without separation,
Maybe I only see what I want to see.

What we are I cannot tell,
A pool of knowledge keeps us bound,
Something reaches for me,
Drawing me to itself.

A connection exists between us all,
Denial demands we remain alone,
Discernment of realities is invisible,
Feelings are our unreliable compasses.

Labels of identification are aloof,
Even our names are fictitious inventions,
We only know what others have taught,
Searching drains our very essence.

Craving dissipates amidst contemplation,
Knowing closes tired eyes,
Connection withdraws its groping tendrils,
Emptiness continues to reign supreme.

Speak

When the hour became great
And darkness folded in,
Ice crystals formed a pedestal
Like glass
For holding a bust in bronze
To be spoken to as living
As if a phantom of memory
Was filling a voided space
For communications to come
As needed.

Always the familiar face,
The one of love's memory
Always attentive to words
Spoken in confidence
Without expectation of judgment;

Missing you is a matter of hurting –
A matter I wish to avoid
I can look upon the bust on the pedestal
Believe a part of your essence is gathered within
As my mind pours forth things wishing to be said
In the privacy of just we two.

Being there
Without being there
Our visions seem to meet
Vigilante as you are
I can sense your caring
I need you to know
And to believe
Love
Did not die.

Future Becomes But Memory

I find a tempest in dew
Rolling its slow dripping balls
The door to Forever Farms closes
I step through in timely demise
Gone is another memory of youth
With only overgrown hints
Satiated in fumes of blackberry ferment
Succulent wine of days past
Drunk seriously with friends and lovers;

I step over Imperium Roses
Now grown wild over fine bricks
Misty air rocks toward fog
Sparrows spring up into eves
Structures darken and crumble
I can hear the dust fall
The way to the trail is carpeted in briars
Sweet is the smell of Dewberry delight
New wild berries taking over
Where rolls my mind into grief
Lost in past visions
A life within my past

A love of belief in forever
But now the nests of home
Are a piece of love having fallen away.

Illusory Chase

I clicked her slick slide to the west
Saw deeper into the blackness of breath
Where dojos held training in belief
Of how souls merged with a taut body

It was my image of her power and quickness
Her heightened sensuality as sacrifice to love
My eyes have followed her lithe movements
Imagination lets her sleep in a lily's embrace

I have seen her in dreams beyond my mind
Heard the voice I recognized without knowing
Locked eyes with a distant image, then
Lost the figure through fences and gates

Her blinking closed the yawning gap
Between rooftops and empty streets
I teetered over dangerous crossings
A 4x6 ramp led me to a pigeon nodding

I heard her voice, felt her breath,
Her hand against my chest in earnest belief
Candlelight flickering in eyes of longing
Thoughts of encompassing her delicate beauty

No matter how fast I ran I couldn't catch her shadow's passing
I threw my head back quickly to catch the jet going by
And fell down dizzy for the effort
Still empty of realizing what I had missed

I craved with a yearning deep inside
Searched for a tidbit of the unknown
Holding out my arms to stumble in the dark
I glimpsed the desperate mark of losing

The missing was as bad as the seeking
How could I find a place to rest?
The holy land of rapid futility engulfed me
Her face faded as she turned away.

A Simple World

Listen to daisies grow
Watching thistle open slow
Tiny moths land
Salamanders eye their prizes
A world within a world
I wish I knew where to lay my head

Maybe one day I could lead a parade
Of happiness lived in joyful exuberance
Reflecting like lights in the sky
In colored masks of
Brightest yellow
Glistening red
Boldest blue
Demure pink –
We could strut in pride
Celebrate smiling
Revel in hugging
Be the simple beings we are.

About the Author

L. C. Fothe was born and raised in New Orleans. His poetry has appeared in various journals over the years. His love of the English language is apparent throughout these works. Bringing upliftment and caring has always been his goal.

www.ingramcontent.com/pod-product-compliance
Lightning Source LLC
LaVergne TN
LVHW041046150826
845672LV00001B/500

* 9 7 9 8 8 4 6 5 7 2 4 1 6 *